WHISPERS OF A DYING SUN

ARCHIVE ZERO | NEW YORK | 2017
www.archivezero.com

Published by Archive Zero, LLC

Zeroth Edition

Paperback ISBN: 978-0-9975442-2-0
E-book ISBN: 978-0-9975442-3-7

Copyright © 2017 Kelvin C. Bias

Cover design by Robson Garcia Jr.
Formatting by Polgarus Studio

Names, characters, places, businesses and incidences either are the product of the author's imagination or used fictitiously, and any resemblance to actual persons, living or dead, businesses, companies, events, or locales is entirely coincidental.

No part of this book may be used or reproduced in any manner without written permission from the author, except in the case of brief quotations embodied in an article or a review.

PUBLISHER'S NOTE

What is Archive Zero?

The name is a combination of archive: a repository or collection especially of information, and zero: (3rd definition) the point of departure in reckoning; more pointedly, the point from which the graduation of a scale (like a thermometer) begins.

When I started my publishing company, I did so with the intent of trying to create a compendium of innovative content for the philosophers of the future. We are the architects.

According to Albert Einstein, any distinction between the past, present, and future is "a stubbornly persistent illusion." So perhaps if what's past is prologue, and the future is now, the present is both past and future, and a zero point phenomenon occurs eternally. Envision all the words for human conditions that would look much better with the word "Zero" in front of it.

War.

Famine.

Poverty.

Homelessness.

Prejudice.

The list could go on, but maybe one day, there will be no need for a list. In another way, my name could be read to mean: Absolute Zero (the Kelvin scale) Prejudice (Bias). Let's approach zero together.

Welcome to Archive Zero.

Kelvin C. Bias

for Kokomi & Momoka

Contents

Publisher's Note iii

Mr. X 1

ARCHIVE THREE 3

Cataclysmic Gumball 5
Chasing Methuselah 6
Crucifixion Of The Upside Down Clown 7
2:22 A.M. 8
2:22 P.M. 9
The Pause Before The Storm 10
Why Do We Have Bombs? 11
Sleeping On The Rings Of Saturn 12
Simultaneous Kiss 13
Mental Masturbation 14
Ascending To Euphoria 15
Lords Of Eternity 16

ARCHIVE TWO 17

Emblem In The Sky 19
Pathos In The Halls Of Eden 20
Underwater Sunset 21

Mathematics 22
Mirror In The Mind's Sky... 23
Symptoms Of Pandemonium 24
Twilight Of The Dawn 25
Gigantic 26
Flux.. 27
I Looked Up In The Sky 28
Tantrum Of The Prophet... 29
Celestial Bodies 31

ARCHIVE ONE 33

Whispers Of A Dying Sun 35
Patchwork Blue 36
Juxtapose The Universe... 37
Proteus.. 38
The Mysterious World Of Ezra P. Zachary 39
The Ends Of The Earth 41
Excerpts From Planet X... 43
The Millennium Dreamer 44
The Congressman 45
Van Gogh's Anti-Insanity Love Tonic 47
The Unborn Sun.. 48
Mission: Earth.. 49
Infinity Cubed 50
Dancing On Mars 51
Wednesday... 52
The Future 53

ARCHIVE ZERO 55

The Final Glance Between Two Lovers At
  The End Of The World 57
Laughing At Alpha Centauri 58
Sunshine Of The Magical Children 59
Mystical Filth 61
Passageway To X 62
Thesaurus Rex 63
Counting Zeros 64
Sabbatical To Saturn 65
Eulogy For The Living 66
To The Parents Of An Unaborted Fetus 67
Microscopic Answers 70
Mind In The Gutter 71
Fluorescent Love 72
Times Of A Clock 73
Threshold Of The Defiant Abyss 74
Nebula 77
I Hold The Universe In My Hands 78

Epilogue 79
Acknowledgements 81
Other Work By Kelvin C. Bias 83
About The Author 85

MR. X

The scientist or his invention,
The condemned man without a name
Or a saint with words too powerful?
The good are always persecuted.
In the future, he will have a title,
But an unknown passport
With one inscription: X.
The laughter of his knowledge
Captures many hearts.
Minds that are malleable.
Before age jades.
The lessons he can teach,
The molecules of wisdom,
Have blessed his soul.
His aura is his gift.
He wants you to know.
He wants to embrace the world.
Mr. X loves you.

ARCHIVE THREE

CATACLYSMIC GUMBALL

Imagine, perchance, that
Inside a 25-cent gumball,
Were the ingredients for doomsday.
Red or blue? Yellow or green?
Ask your mother.
Within this cataclysmic gumball
A five-year old boy holds the galactic key,
The fate of the universe in his hands,
Holding the pearl of all pearls,
Mother Earth at his disposal.
Would you be afraid?
Should you be afraid?
Not until he becomes an adult,
And the bombings begin.

CHASING METHUSELAH

The eroded man ends his temperate cheer,
Leaning to the side of his rocking chair.
A grumbled term is
A last ditch effort at salvation.
The words he longed to say,
The words that haunt him still.
Healing did not time his wounds.
The prospect of death proved the salve.
Grief, he says, is no answer.
Loose change is forgotten in the end,
Meaningless possibilities.
As his head droops and the pulse stops,
A final sound is heard:
"I'm…."

CRUCIFIXION OF THE UPSIDE DOWN CLOWN

A martyr of laughter. The cause.
His words futile in the face of ignorance.
Foreign jests, not his own, and courts
Subvert the truth.
Making all things beautiful, ugly.
Lords of the vale preclude grace.
A fountain will dry up in the tyranny.
The outcome of his demise,
Leads to war. Kill the funny man.
He is a threat.
When the people listen,
Those in power will destroy him.
Intelligence beyond humor.
The kingdom will suffer.
So say the architects of chaos.
They don't want giggling.
They've got a war to start.
So put the clown on the cross.
His words can hurt them no more.
But his memory holds greater power.

2:22 A.M.

The world spins on its axis.
Other worlds spin on theirs.
Celestial clockwork.
The rhythm of us,
From the stardust of our birth.
A great continent bridges
Our souls to outer space.
A time. A place. A moment.
2:22
And all is well.

2:22 P.M.

The conjunction of three entities:
Our heart, our mind and our soul.
At the precise second of union,
The skies open and look down.
At the same Earth.
The same ocean.
The same people.
Join in the peace the similarity holds.
Join in the everyday celebration.
It is 2:22 everywhere.

THE PAUSE BEFORE THE STORM

The light at the end of the tunnel
Needs somebody to turn it on.
Is it you or I?
Where do our thoughts go in the calm?
Without doubt, there is no certainty.
A posse of posers instills a lot.
You have to decide,
Which follower to lead.
Eradicate the desperate folks.
Make your own syndicate.
And blink before you take over.
The world will not wait.
Let it rain hard.
Your storm
Bleeds its own blood.
Let the preparation begin.

WHY DO WE HAVE BOMBS?

The U.N. diplomat walks to the podium
And addresses the nations
Portraying his notion of divine retribution and
Posing only one question: five words
Why do we have bombs?

They serve no earthly purpose.
No consternation is great enough to defy.
The heads of state putting their heads together
With the weapons of mass destruction
Resting between them. Decidedly dumb.

Countries make plans within plans with aplomb
The speech is the longest in assembled history
Yet when all is said and done. Nothing.
A collection of rhetoric subsides calmly
Until a white-hot flash and black rain.

SLEEPING ON THE RINGS OF SATURN

Want to join me? The view is spectacular.
The colors radiant and cold. The icy void.
A pedestal of imagination.
There is no here or there,
No how or why, only pure existence.
Not a monument, but a wellspring of reveries.
The delicate rings have a gift,
A call to mind as you sleep.
Dreaming of crystal fantasies
Of an extinct civilization,
The masters of the atom.
The exquisitely shaped molecules,
Banter between the worlds.
As I rest to create,
The planet pulls. And I slumber.

SIMULTANEOUS KISS

A warm embrace, followed by meshed lips.
Thoughts, words, and passions: transferred.
In an instant, the world falls away.
Electric transmissions are the residue.
We suspect the lifeblood, flowing,
Rising and concentrating.
Each of the other in one another.
A touch becomes an epoch.
And twirling fantasies take hold.
The spirit in the middle of us
Is the center of the galaxy,
A singing black hole.
The octave of desire.
Think about the moment.
We can play B flat forever.
Glean all that you can.
For the lessons of a kiss
Are simultaneously drawn.

MENTAL MASTURBATION

Language, dental floss for the intellects.
Periods and exclamation points
For the blackboard poets.
The armies of youth of the future.
Devise their plan and follow it.
Instead of an aftermath,
A prologue to the rally of fear.
What they say, we'll bear in mind.
Scribbles on a sheet of papyrus
Contain the same intent.
Eons later, they won't understand.
Spell it out clearly.
Make a labyrinth of the outcome,
And the ancestors of Adam won't know
The reason we failed.
Mental masturbation is what you choose.

ASCENDING TO EUPHORIA

Straight toward the promised intent.
Happiness is all-powerful.
A blasphemy is destroyed.
The air up here is succulent.
A juicy potion for the satiated lords.
Bedlam suddenly arises.
Cymbals crash and focus the eyes.
On the fireworks of love.
The brilliant light display.
A charter elevator direct to Cloud 9.
Portals of space and time intersect,
Where we envision and manifest.
The resurrection will occur.
Beam me up.

LORDS OF ETERNITY

Across the eye of the void,
The lords gallop toward destiny,
Painted in amazing tinctures:
Turquoise, emerald, garnet.
Their path in the universe leaps.
It is not cut in stone,
But etched by human hands.
Entering the dream of mortal men,
They shed their tears and appear.
Infantile reasoning is not the law.
The mystical forces guide themselves.
We follow their clock,
But write our own laws.
Standing guard, the rules bind them.
They cannot intervene.
We decide our fate.
Yet with each passing sunset,
The countdown continues.
As the sky's hues blend into forever,
We ponder the ways of the watcher,
Seeking an entrance into their souls
To achieve the greatest gift.
We choose. We accomplish. We burn.
We are the arsonists.
The lords of eternity are our guides.

ARCHIVE TWO

EMBLEM IN THE SKY

The nobles with superior technology
Will arrive one day, teaching us something,
Forcing us to reveal our fragile hearts,
Arriving with the force to crush us.
They will be called the atmospheric enemy.
Our native leaders gather and shun reason.
Press the button! Press the button!
We are weak and they are strong.
Destroy our planet; we are experts.
And suddenly, the alien awakened.
His nightmare unrealized.
Supplanted by the fear of Earth.
The ones who will end it all.
The prophecy of the universe.
The bombs rip the fabric of time.
The emblem in the sky,
The atomic end to innocence
Came long ago. We cannot go back.
There we have it. Let it pass.
But don't let it lie. Defend.
Heal the searing flames we have wrought.
The end is only the beginning.

PATHOS IN THE HALLS OF EDEN

The monuments of jesting justice
Beckon to the lesser of two evils.
A crying soul wails under the strain.
Banished by the unloved, the loved wander,
Through fields of bodies, overturned and sacred.
There, in the cornerstone of civilization,
The seedlings for a bright future need protection.
Underneath a cloud of judgment, a man wilts.
His essence bears the weight of nations.
Chaos, fire and destruction will last seven days.
And then a new realization comes to pass.
It shall be engraved in the minds of all people.
The final reckoning, a testament to the quest.
A search for lasting peace.
Pathos in the halls of Eden will abate.
When?

UNDERWATER SUNSET

Behold a brightness beyond dreams.
A soothing light from the land of spirits.
The place that is understood.
A miraculous journey of the sun,
So powerful, you cannot fathom escape.
The gleaming glint and passionate release.
The atomic energy, a thousand fold,
Where the paths of angels are laid.
Amidst the rays, a floating goddess
Moves forward to meet her destiny.
The peaceful maker, the truth seeker,
Aligning her body with the underwater sunset.

MATHEMATICS

Beyond the furthest reaches of sanity,
Beneath the heaviest debt of sin,
A bandit seeks you out. A wizard.
You are the pupil of the ancient.
His sorcery belies your understanding.
Yet terrored, the notion of his wisdom blinds.
A shaman of infinite knowledge.
The mystical one plies his wares.
He lays down precepts.
You can only heed them, he says.
And a man's parable of beliefs follows:
Don't let the lessons become the lesser.
Don't let the blessing become blasphemy.
Don't let the future become a regretted past.
Simple mathematics: an equation for serenity.
As the elder leaves you by the wayside,
The message is a hymn from heaven.
Hear it again.

MIRROR IN THE MIND'S SKY
(inspired by Rene Magritte's *The False Mirror*)

What do you see when an infinite sky looks at you?
Your reflection, wise inflection, contemplation?
In this sea, you see what you perceive:
A mirror in the eye's mind.
A dark planet overcome by bliss.
A never-ending blue that looks backward at you and smiles.
Like a lover's glance just before a fallen tear
Or a gentle breeze moving islands, your innermost desires.
Along the edges, there is nowhere to hide.
You look into the air, and all you see is you.
Pastel hues. Is it true?
Clouds destined for perpetuity.

SYMPTOMS OF PANDEMONIUM

A panoply of passionate peculiars,
All rolled into a systematic ball.
A function of the divergence of saints.
Processed, we all notice the change.
The crashing of cymbals like ocean waves.
A strong finish in the bat of an eyelid.
A loud noise that never dissipates.
In the singularity of a vacuum,
The voice of reason has no name.
The vibrations of sounds are the lexicon.
The symptoms of the rhythmic drummer.
A perfect translation and intimidation of thought.
The definite peace. The prelude to true chaos.
Pray for glee. Pray for the pandemonium.

TWILIGHT OF THE DAWN

The pretense of the ages mediates,
Winding its way across the astral sea.
Concentrating its graceful effort
On the first moments of time.
In the sweetness of memory,
The sun will rise again and again.
Her horizon lit by a surreal fire,
The saints of luminosity in
An age of extreme bliss,
A kiss for the ancestors to bear.
We are all toddlers amongst the stars.
Gladly breathing purified air.
United, we welcome the light.

GIGANTIC

From the top of an ice peak on Callisto
The space giant conducts his sermon,
Hoping someone will heed his words.
"We must create bliss," he bellows
Beyond Neptune, outward past Pluto and into infinity.
"Declare war on the inane and pacify the stars," he utters.
His green eyes glower a billion miles past the edge of space.
With a giant arm, he aligns the planets one by one. Earth is last.
And the last won't be first because
They already destroyed their garden.
After the earthlings climbed into their spaceships and vanished,
Looking for new worlds to conquer and abuse,
The behemoth watcher shed tears
And melted Europa's frozen sea.
"We need more petroleum."
Suddenly a wormhole opens in space without time,
A bright light, then a new planet emerges.
Planet X is here. And we would have revered.
But we are not there. The giant looks up and smiles.
Maybe next time, we'll obey his wishes.

FLUX

The deluxe demon, an inner space missive, forms the nucleus.
A battered diamond bombarded by shells sleeps inside.
Distant worlds lie on the horizon of another dimension.
A light cuts a swath through the rivers of molecular activity.
Zero degrees at an altitude of zero. An imaginary pole.
Decisions are made on this spectral plane, seducing gravity.
Parity arrives when the solemn force meets anti-matter
In a centrifuge. Down the spiral of universal proportions:
Flux. Redux. An altered state of being. Higher consciousness.
A ripped dress in the fabric of time leads us to an answer.

I LOOKED UP IN THE SKY

A blast of wind caressed my torso,
And directed my thoughts toward you.
As the twilight reflected my soul,
The myriad emotions floated endlessly.
Up to the heavens, into eternity.
The stars and their brethren are home.
Can the weight of sorrow overcome?
The burden of sacrifice for your essence.
The battle fought far in the realm of space.
Gazing skyward, I entertain 1,000 angels.
Laughing, a tear streams down my face.
The terror continues: war, pestilence and fear.
The end of the blessed, the flipside of bliss.
It all circulates brilliantly as I watch.
Unknowing, the sky looks down at me.

TANTRUM OF THE PROPHET

Words are the trumpet of the steel-eyed wanderer.
His shield: the wailing of a madman.
The one who saw tomorrow, today.
As he yells atop the pillar of knowledge,
The screams hurtle toward you.
At speeds that elicit the fear of death.
The great orator announces his plan.
The feeble minds don't listen.
Heed the thoughts and brace yourself.
The magnitude of the cryptic cynic.
Creeps toward the edge of sanity.
No one believes him.
But his words ring true.
A mastermind's game, dazzling visions.
Pinpointed in the corners of the brain.
The place where nobody listens.
Enraged, the elder convulses.
We let the Earth bleed!
We let heaven weep!
We let life ooze away!
Heed my predictions!
I am the prophet!
And suddenly,
The wind stops.

And silence reigns.
The town crier resurrected.
Judgment Day is here.
Standing before us.
We judge the prophet.
None of them came true.
As a dove flutters past,
Into the still, lucid air.
He replies gently smiling,
"They weren't supposed to."

CELESTIAL BODIES

In the midst of each other's eternity.
Beyond the happenstance and nonsense of a used world.
Where forever is shared, touches are exchanged and nothing dies.
Each particle in our essence equates its own purpose,
Rising with the swirl of a million planets—all with life.
On their own Nazca Lines, the runways of von Däniken
Manifest themselves in wormholes and black holes.
Leading to nebulas and frozen worlds in the void.
As I grab your hand, we float past Planet X.
At one with the universe we weave together.
Holding fast to the idea that all things exist.
And co-exist here: the formation of creation.
The beginning of the beginning. We see it simultaneously.
Complete consciousness with science.
We communicate without speaking.
Think without thinking, and by osmosis, we love.
As we continue, we ruminate amongst greater stars.
By waving our hands, we cause a waterfall of beautiful gases,
Which in turn twirl into pools of life: building blocks.
The sounds meld into hearts, collecting the knowledge of epic dreams.
So far in the entirety, we see the universal trigonometry,
The reasons for the reasons and for the mystery.
Globes within globes within globes as melodies fill our lobes.
From large to small and beyond infinity,

Pleasures and passions merge at the center of this magical journey.
We see ourselves old; we see ourselves young.
All in a millennial blink.
Special insights form in our brains
As we witness the coming tide of destiny.
The paragon of palatial fantasies shapes our moves. We go willingly.
The exquisite beauty of what we can't see.
Our celestial bodies.

ARCHIVE ONE

WHISPERS OF A DYING SUN

Lamented, lost and leery,
The vestiges of light crawl across the sea.
Searching for a home.
A kaleidoscope under a microscope,
Transforms the horizon into eternity.
As we blink, the shards become shorter,
Unable to kill us with their beauty.
The scientists sigh and hope for revival.
A final breath, and then a silent painless death.
Darkness is upon us.

PATCHWORK BLUE

A spread of color in the desert.
A sewn button on a mangled shirt.
Squares interspersed with circles.
The dirty laundry of a wanderer
Knows no boundaries.
The sky above is the closest kin.
A patchwork blue. A mended tear.
The arrogance of the spectrum
Intimidates the shades of gray.
A matrix is a friend.
Unity.
Look within.

JUXTAPOSE THE UNIVERSE

Replace energy with totality.
A pure essence of everything.
The effort greater than,
Hercules twirling the rings of Saturn.
Place the atomic power of the Sun
Into your heart, and
Shine the brightest light on yourself.
Upend the tyranny of oppression,
Filling it with the hope of the stars.
Masses of gases hold the potential.
The key to a new understanding.
We can reverse all negativity.
Nebulas, quasars and comets.
The building blocks of tomorrow.
Juxtapose the universe.
And tell a friend.

PROTEUS

The blue sphere of a distant world.
Spinning in its own corner of space.
Our twin. Our watery sepulcher.
We will come one day.
To join the faces of the world.
To bridge the gap and learn.
To end our mistakes and fix theirs.
Vice versa. The leader, Plaxon says.
The council meets and Naxos arrives.
The two leaders colonize the mind.
Reaching a climax all can agree on.
A puzzle they will solve together.
And the waterfalls of Proteus,
Will never run dry.
A jubilant scale is nigh.
Civilizations united in celebration.
The creatures of and from the sea.
Two spheres live on.

THE MYSTERIOUS WORLD OF EZRA P. ZACHARY

Bound in his straightjacket in an 1883 Wyoming jail,
Ezra P. Zachary has only one option: his imagination.
He went to Paris three times last week
And well past Mars and into Jupiter's orbit
Only twenty seconds ago.
You see as he sits in his special corner,
He defiantly devises new destinations and desires.
Ol' miners say they can feel ol' Ezra P. in their thoughts
When they are deep in the Montana hills
Searching for the new pot at the end of a bow of rain.
Seventy-eight years old and counting.
"I'm gonna live to 102!"
There is a yell from the back of the cell.
Ezra P. determined with glee.
Chuckles. He just witnessed a desolate
Killing. The focal point of his brain's lens
A cowboy died at White Sands today.
The deliverer, bringer of bad news.
He had been there once back in 1862. A renegade then.
He was there again today. From the back of his cell
He settled an old score.
The constant drip of water feeding his fuel as he

Stares in the glint of the kerosene lamp
And is transported back, seeing himself as a young man
Without the grey beard or cragged face.
No windows—only steel bars and a jailer's key.
His stare becomes more intent; his glare more focused.
Ezra P. is no longer there.
He knows, but we don't.
He is talking to himself…in 1805.
And now, some miners sing an ode to Ezra P.

THE ENDS OF THE EARTH

The classified pulse of high places
Surrounds the magnanimous faces
Without names. Atom's Apple radiates
Across the ocean blue. As we mix
Our flammable liquids. And grow
White hair and chase zeros
And buy 10 item's or less at Lucky's.
When hell freezes over, there will be
A war in Hollywood. A timebomb.
On Avenue X, fear itself runs with blue dogs.
And all the dirty laundry is revealed.
South of the border bluebloods hunt their young.
Killing Cain is the speeding bullet of history.
Mindless 12-year-old boys in Illinois dictate
TV policy with their lust for sanguine delights.
While in the background love is the
Uncatchable fish that cuts to the bone.
Life: a roadmap of the soul. Going hot.
Some pray to a five o'clock Jesus.
The great American drifters can hear
Eden calling and go into the wild.
We all want to be king for a day.
Or maybe not in the first days of embryonic
Dreams. Greener pastures do lie in wait,

A canvas for the five-leaf clover.
The boardroom where gods reign supreme and
Exact revenge on things left unsaid.
In the name of love, we take our first steps.
And suddenly say our last words
As it all comes to a dramatic end.

EXCERPTS FROM PLANET X

Fantastic transmissions emanate from the tenth planet,
The undiscovered orb that travels in a mischievous orbit.
The green and blue hues of the spectrum disperse
And are disclosed in the astral projection of Zeus.
Tablets of stone circulate under cirrus clouds.
The terrestrial surface breathes life into carbon,
Dating itself with machinations of an electric empire.
Meanwhile, the ancient rulers meet in council
Deciding the fate of the world and when...
It will meet ours. Can we be trusted?
Does the wormhole of our minds need to be bridged?
Back into the black hole of the unknown, the rings settle.
Around the ball of gas, sparkling ice crystals.
Titan was once our lovely satellite. A friend.
But after the interstellar war, we disappeared
Surfacing on the third rock from our sun.
Planet X is our home. We long for it still.
When we return, it will be the center of the universe,
The place where alien humans alienate Earth.
From there, we go back to ground zero.

THE MILLENNIUM DREAMER

In the year 3000, will there still be
A place called Earth in a galaxy
Known as the Milky Way?
Or will we be on the planet Naxos
Planning the next revolution?
I dream of an enduring Earth.
Where cows will still be milked
By a 48-year-old farmer in Kansas
And there will still be fireworks
On the Fourth of July.
Beneath a fire lit sky, we shall celebrate not
Just the U.S., but the world. All
Peace will ring true. Danger a long absent
Concept *and* precept.
A myth we all strive to understand.
The pathos subsides as one person stands alone,
One who transcends the diapers of nations.
The millennium dreamer waves her flag.

THE CONGRESSMAN

Spastic regurgitations of the noble kind
Transfix the plainest of speeches.
As the congressman guides lunatics to allow
Stringently stupid laws, he is beholden to others
With more firepower than his constituents,
People he has never met,
People the Party controls,
People that can't spell your name.
Or point to Iraq on a map. Maybe Nebraska.
Guns, Guns, Guns.
The congressman liked guns
Until he was gunned down in front
Of the U.S. Capitol by a six-year-old
Who found his father's gun under the bed,
Whom the congressman would contend had
"Watched too much TV".
A resident of the gated community,
Gunville. Don't we all feel at home?
Our home on the range
In the land of the free, home of the strange
A land where Hollywood is always named.
The next kid's parents paid him no attention,
And didn't even own a gun.
He bought it at school.

So who is really to blame?
I say, his replacement: "The Congressman....
Please vote for me."

VAN GOGH'S ANTI-INSANITY LOVE TONIC

There is no cure for the world's best disease.
Chocolate. Candy. Caffeine. Three "C's" never ceasing.
A peace. A piece. Replace the absinthe.
Slicing off the ear is a little extreme, but
If that's what you feel. Try to do it bloodlessly.
Arles is beautiful in the spring.

There is no disputing the fact that
Cherries still blossom after George told a lie.
Brainwaves of a schizophrenic,
I'm only a messenger. Don't shoot me.
Read between the lines and curl your head back.
The words may take over, a long-awaited rebellion

Restrained by a genius' gift with the brush.
Strokes radiantly aspire to assemble beauty,
Achieving the highest honors on the wall of fame.
Musee D'Orsay. The Louvre. A gallery in the skull.
Deep in the synapses of the gifted.
And what we try to achieve. And exalt.

THE UNBORN SUN

Twinkles in a cold spatial existence
A collection of dust and gas swirling
Into a cohesive nuclear smile
That shines apart from the void
And upsets the balance of chaos
From which it is born. Unscorned,
The newborn spirals clearly to an undivided path.
Circling the spherical mind of the creator.
The androgynous creature waves its hand
Melting the abstract abyss into a singularity
Beguiling us with its call to glow.
A minister speaks to the sequined universal squire.
Rays, shafts and neon barter their way inside
Cleansing the roof of heaven on the flyby.

MISSION: EARTH

The last drop of a decaying civilization
Reverberates through the ionic transformer.
As the looming monolith nears her target,
A chromatic alien bends her fingers,
Training the eye to see light in a different way.
Blips and bleeps flash inside the metallic core
And cries of yesterdays past fill the radar screen.
A time capsule unfreezes. Undaunted,
A robot thaws it for consumption.
Manipulated and mesmerized, the data
Leads to one conclusion. No delusion.
The planet kicked us off. And we went
To the deep outer reaches
Only to return for mourning,
And discover we weren't alone
In the mission to transform Earth.

INFINITY CUBED

The passageway leads to a door that opens
into another Universe and leads to a bigger door.
That door in turn leads to a smaller door at the
End of a black hole that eats itself like Ouroboros.
The time-space continuum is dashed in this arena.
A spectacle of atomic dust and bowling-ball-sized molecules
Conspire to form another solar system,
Protons, electrons, gravitons, neutrons.
Fused together into nothingness, and
Then smashed again. The rings of Saturn are
Pockets of resistance, the keys to worlds.
The plan of the almighty jester, who laughs
Her way into the conundrum at the edge of existence.
The stars wave at us as we pass.
From there we are on our own.
On our way to the third ring of infinity.

DANCING ON MARS

The red surface tinged with habitations of a long extinct civilization.
A parallel culture spinning out of control,
Bombarded by the exterior calm.
Beneath the permafrost, remnants of life persist,
Hidden by the path of the unknown caretaker.
Where did the Martians go?
We are the ones soaking up their last dance,
Cavorting on the rocky terrain,
Dividing hope from sorrow, the quick from the dead.
Searching for the superhighway from Solis Lacus to Olympus Mons,
The volcano queen bigger than any other in the stellar neighborhood.
A monstrous sight, daunting in its stark obesity.
The radio of Phobos and Deimos plays a harmony.
The men in the white suits begin to step in line.
They are the first ones there.
Put on another song.

WEDNESDAY

Love is made.
Beds are tucked in joy.
A child asks a mother an innocent question,
Receiving a not so banal answer.
Daffodils rise to meet the sun.
Birds call to their brethren.
Flocks flock amongst the deer.
The woods echo in silence
And caress your ear.
Today is the day.
A powerful day.
The day we lie in ecstasy under a moonlight sky.
Sing praises to the lord of the forest.
And preach prudence to the squirrels
Wherever they are.
A church of aspens,
A cathedral of firs,
A temple of grass,
Made a village by the river they all share.
Wednesday we will be there.

THE FUTURE

Visions of apocalyptic doom disintegrate
In this pristine wilderness of the unknown.
There are no horsemen, only sinners and their sins.
Saints and their sanctity, and mercy.
The invisible whirl of a thousand lifetimes,
Dissected and salved. Possessions remain.
Thoughts link Earth with the stars,
An interconnected fragment of steel,
Left as a monument to the past,
The opposite of the present and
The inverse of the forgotten miles tread.
Dreams multiply at the speed of light.
Cathartic rings of a supple candle's glow
Stream through the open window of
The young man's soul.
Eternal youth is a robot.
The future walks backward into the sun.
Electric angels follow with Wi-Fi.
Saturn communicates with Neptune and vice versa.
As the tiny speck of a planet as we know it
Lets out manufactured breaths,
We are artificially inseminated.
Traveling down an uncharted road.

ARCHIVE ZERO

THE FINAL GLANCE BETWEEN TWO LOVERS AT THE END OF THE WORLD

The flash before the flash.
A fleeting instant that lasts beyond eternity.
Before the eyes are sealed in doom
1,000 words are exchanged.
Telepathically transmitted in a blink
Without any need for explanation.
Many lives can be lived in one second,
Or even two or three.
But only one matters,
The one you want to see.

The final thoughts etched in the mind.
However, no one else will ever know.
The end of the world is nigh.
Don't let the final glance be your last.
Let it reside somewhere in the hereafter
Where heaven and earth collide and share.
And all things are bared.
Behind a wizard's fallen curtain,
The essence of meaning is sacrificed
As our lovers unite and disappear.

LAUGHING AT ALPHA CENTAURI

Way out there…
A wave travels without being heard.
A signal maintained at a constant pitch.
Delayed for years as it streaks.
It's rhythmic vibration, heading on a collision course
Toward the people of Earth, from the people of the stars.
The ones we can't see. The ones Arecibo can't hear.
But we know they are there
Smiling back at us and wondering too,
Are we alone?
Are we all there is?
Brown-eyed creatures exist everywhere.
Across the void all things are possible.
And soon we will know.
That people are laughing beyond Alpha Centauri.

SUNSHINE OF THE MAGICAL CHILDREN

Twirling within their own mind
Happy, pure and free
Laughing constantly in the backseat
Of mom and dad's 1977 Dodge Aspen.
On the way to Niagara Falls
Waiting to cause havoc,
Or bite their teacher and get their
Sixth birthday taken away.
But be smart enough to know
That happiness comes in other
Packages. Disneyland, it doesn't
Have to be. In one swift motion a
Five-year-old boy can suddenly
Be in the sunshine of his own
Magic kingdom. Advocating
Grins and cooties and…
Frogs….yes, I said frogs.
A child sees the true beauty of the creature,
And a black splotch on the sidewalk
Or the twinkle of a whiskey-named cat's eye.
And the viability of dancing in a cemetery.
They agree on the merits

Of their make-believe friend.
Snuffleupagus is the man.
Or maybe he's asexual, but
The magical ones don't need
To know that. In fact, it doesn't
Matter to them....fun and games
And shiny new toys...G.I. Joe or Barbie.
Or an upside down Christmas tree
With fake snow on it if you live in L.A.,
And strive for what you don't have,
Surfing on a 10-foot wave as the setting sun
Dips into the blue water and reacts to the sky,
Exploding in orange, pink and all shades
Of the spectrum that aren't black.
Kids, kids, kids, having fun with an ashtray.
Patient because they have so much to keep them occupied
In the land of wild things
And speak to themselves in the Magic Mirror,
Waiting for daddy to come home and latch
Onto his size 12 foot and get taken for a ride,
Not knowing that one day they will
Have to manufacture this feeling, trying to keep
The innocence they once had, when they frolicked and
Played. Played by the world, playing within it
Keeping all delicate objects in a special place
Before they finally settle
Into the sunset of a wrinkled, pondering brain.

MYSTICAL FILTH

The dispensed valve of dreamland's material waste
Vibrates against the leg of the scientific totem pole,
Emanating pandemic pleasures for the senses.
A green odor permeates the ultimate sweets,
Groping for the strands of pubescent effort.
The illicit beats pander to the lowest brain
As masters of their own domain dwindle.
The discarded scum is rounded up,
Molded into a ball and then processed.
Out comes the perfect gestation. A powerful
Strain of equalized asphalt from those in command.
We consume it everyday and grow into the super being.

PASSAGEWAY TO X

A fantastic spectacle lies before us.
Ionian strains of ancient civilizations lead the way.
Circuitry long since ceased, but droning again.
Clockwork hands, pointing into the stars, peer
Through the telescope of an alien race.

The spasms caused by outrageous discovery
Ravish the world with anarchy and chaos.
Fears mount from the doubting governments,
Fighting over the next occupant of greatness.
A hollow tube we want to exploit, rejuvenate.

Within the tomb of bliss, peace lurks.
We must join forces, fuse these fragments.
Building a bridge to the moon is no easy task.
The departed ancestors left us their gift.
A passageway to X, not a death sentence.

THESAURUS REX

Protean beings flirt frequently when they are fomented.
The apogee of adoration imperils no one. Serial serenity.
Though convoked in convoluted coruscation
To requite the ulterior fiend. Crawling toward the sky,
The sassy monster sighs, satiated by the flames of rapture.
A mighty creature with onyx oodles of oomph.
Undenied, it beckons for a new master.
We feed him with words: utterances, remarks, statements.
Comments vociferated from the mountaintop.
His command of the language is a pinnacle
Only reached by a meandering road of distinct divinity.
Depression cursed away by a knowing kind.
Osculating ameliorates the situation, staunching any wound.
Your desire is laid bare in the presence of the beast.

COUNTING ZEROS

Businessmen in three-piece suits,
A homeless man in Washington Square Park
And bankers on the backside, beneath solace,
We are all adding up our zeros,
Pinching our pennies, making our next move,
Collecting dust. Editing ourselves. And
Not letting thoughts flow fast and free.
The sky reigns over the greed of capitalism.
Gold, frankincense and myrrh are not enough.
Skyscrapers must go higher, further, wider.
Bridges to every indigenous culture.
Please sir, would you like another?

SABBATICAL TO SATURN

Wilting under the sun's glare in St. Tropez
I decide to astral project my mind
To the icy rings of the outer planet.
My body wants to stay on the Riviera.
Can you blame it? The misty lee.
In the blink of a second, I fly
Like a transistor radio outward,
Greeting the dawn mightily.
I needed a break from thought so
Camping out on the brown clouds of gas
Seemed rather nice. A pleasant welcome.
Or a planned respite to opposing forces.
Daily, we can go there and anywhere.
Though not all of us do.
From time to time and to be sublime,
Everyone needs a sabbatical to Saturn.

EULOGY FOR THE LIVING

Why does someone have to die for words to sink in?
Our guilty conscience does us no good until it's too late.
Words mean more when the person they're meant for isn't here.
We should listen to our souls talking to us…warning us.
Eulogies for the living can affect change.

Wrap the loved one's being into everyone's core.
Don't wait for death. Embrace existence. Care.
Picture a world where everyone follows this rule:
If everyone knew someone in every other country,
The prospects for war would approach zero.

Peace would expand exponentially,
A clear prism that projects an eternal vision.
The path is the message. The message is the word.
Do you hear them?
They hear you.

TO THE PARENTS OF AN UNABORTED FETUS

Hate?
There is no
Hate for things
Unknown:
The tarried tapestry
Of umbilical aspirations.
Where are you now?
Are your biological clocks
Still ticking?
The mystery of life
Perpetually ground.
To the little one and
Things missed:
Speed Racer,
Sesame Street,
The love for Super Grover,
DNA transmitted or
An adopted time-felt
Memory displaced.
A life that could
Have been;
A life that is

Genetically advanced.
Flesh from flesh,
Conceived in a
Summer of Love.
'69 questions to ask.
Future, present and past
Connected by the
Cord of curiosity
That overwhelms
The lost ones.
Who are they?
I don't know.
Do I look like
Them and they
Like me?
Given away
At the day of
Three—
A life recycled
That begins anew.
Place of birth
At the hospital
Of Angels.
A baby
Brought into
This world
Crying for the
Gods of the Scream
Until he's picked

Up in gentle hands and declared:
The Most Beautiful Baby at the Baby Store.
On the third day he dreams.
Grateful, no less,
Avoiding aborted
Asylum and running
Toward fear.
A tear may be
Shed, but
Never recycled.
Unless the
Meeting of one
Plus two.
But, shaking hands
With my face,
There
Is
Only
Love.

MICROSCOPIC ANSWERS

Parallel impressions in another allocation,
Between this world and the next,
A blip on an atom's radar,
Revolving in the mind of our inner self,
The destination we all seek,
The cow we all milk.
We lie fertile on a sea of tranquility,
Seeking knowledge on a tiny rock
In a vast universe with countless sights
And brains and bending spatial flights.
This destination is not final,
But an invitation and a communication,
The place where microchips go to die
In the mind of their Creator. Us.

MIND IN THE GUTTER

Sensationalistic perversions emit crude destiny,
Saturating sadistic proclivities and satirical nonsense.
Wash it off; it'll get dirty down there.
Picking up new concepts and patterns,
The synapses will fire anew and glow.
Ballistic missives aimed at all those who are against them
To shoot down perfect sense.
Curvaceous, we all eventually wander.
Recalling the facts we don't know and
The people who have bent them backward.
Together, without thinking, all blasphemy is
Eventually ignored by the holy rollers.
And a clock strikes itself and others
Pinpointing the precise moment,
When deviant illusions begin.
Awestruck at the peril that can't be envisioned,
The maker meets her master, knowing that
This particular brand of inanity will continue.

FLUORESCENT LOVE

Shining: a neon sign for all to see.
The passionate potentate pursues a pill.
Pushing purple posies into the electric socket.
The capsule makes everything glow.
A phosphorescent, radioactive being
Begins to take over. Ending ills.
A multi-colored flash of brilliance,
There is no stronger aura.
The feeling instilled by the small device
Overcomes all distances and dimensions.
A brightness shinier than a newly minted penny,
A parcel of time magnified a thousand times,
And beacons of verisimilitude, all equal
The triple pinnacles of passion, empathy and bliss.
More striking than all the lights of Vegas,
The simple magic between two eyes
Is the true essence of all that transpires,
The ultimate thought, a penultimate chance.

TIMES OF A CLOCK

Twice upon a time,
A vast tower held the key
To the universe, the hourglass
That held everything together.
Atop this tower, there were two mighty hands,
Ticking and tocking
And rocking the masses.
Glaring across the human square,
The gathering place, like a
Grandfather peering at a newborn heir.
Every hour, without fail, a bell would sail,
Its waves gliding through the pleasant air,
Continuing to circle the globe,
Reminding us all that nothing stands still.
Defying logic, we continue to go.
The clock bellows, "I have a life too!"
No more, no less. Significant.
Elegant and intrinsic,
Two hands make one face: unity.

THRESHOLD OF THE DEFIANT ABYSS

I

The brink of eternity lies ahead.
Behind, the ghost of past transgressions.
Choose your footsteps carefully in the wind.
She will tell you how to transcend immortality.
At the edge of the edge, don't lose yours
Or the defiant abyss will swallow you whole
Like Jonah, in the belly of a whale. You, pale.
Look toward the perpetual horizon, aiming the
Knowledge of every living creature that has
Existed throughout time. A wink in the fabric
Of the universe is the divining rod for ferocious armies.
Thousands of feet below, the souls of lost searchers
Seek the wisdom that will set them free.
Let's throw them into the endless ditch,
Making martyrs of no one, meting out the
Punishment we all so richly deserve.
Save yourself from the precipice.
Save us all from the untold horror.

II

I look up from the startling bottom of the bottomless hole,
Realizing I am at the top of someone else's schism.
Words swirl in this cesspool of chaos,
Screaming tantalizing inspirations.
Grapes are dangled in front of my lips. Shall I take them?
I look down to see countless devices,
All aimed at the warlike center we call Earth.
They prepare their tomb,
Possessing zero zest for the parameters we call laws.
The animated gatekeepers try to push me one way or the other.
Not right nor left or even up and down, but light versus dark.
We must withstand so all of us as I's can remain a collective we.

III

The panic sets in; the abyss grows.
The shrieks of fallen trespassers echo ad infinitum.
The desperate souls claw their way back to the plane of peace,
A temporal zone where dreams meld with reality.
Satisfied demons cry tears of joy
Especially when you have made the wrong decision.
Lying within the prism between chasms, there is suffering.
The vision of the world is a distant memory as you try
To find the medium. The talismans all point sideways.
Steps three and four were sidestepped with frenzy.
No mind in the matter to write the prophecy down.

Bely the hope of the saints and carry passion with you.
That is your sole redemption, a chance at salvation.
Know before you step away from the ledge.
I'll join you there: awakened.

NEBULA

A hot-blooded interstellar being,
Curator of infinite knowledge.
Survives. The most beautiful sight
In the cosmos.
An eagle formed of hydrogen and dust,
Incubators of the stars.
The precious element of dreams
Surpasses space's deepest regions.
Cobalt, white and shades of pink.
Configured into the dazzling core of shadows,
The unicorn between the galaxies,
The nebula watches us and
Lets life live.

I HOLD THE UNIVERSE IN MY HANDS

I hold the universe in my hands.
Skinned knees and boys are distant lighthouses,
moored on foggy shores.
We are alone on nearer seas
in the clear darkness under a singular moon.
The Future dangles from a constellation of radiant plastic stars.
Streetlight slithers into a fantastic array
as taxis and drunken revelers rendezvous on Second Avenue
beneath their own piece of the night.
Shallow breaths power the engines of love.
There are no predators in the shadows.
I possess the power of Zeus.
I am a statue: my fingers and your tiny limbs
meld into a sculptor's curve while we
dream of milk bottles and cherry blossoms
at the base of Fujiyama.
A meteor streaks across the room.
Big sister's cherubic face peers past a cracked door,
a curious angel, to make sure Father Time still ticks.
Family is important, oka-san says, and the little one emits a coo
gentle enough to make all of our hearts burst.
And the hands of the universe hold us in return.

EPILOGUE

THE ANSWER

Love.

ACKNOWLEDGEMENTS

Thank you to my family, which supersedes all the problems in the world. Thank you to anyone who has ever written, read or listened to a poem, and to those of you who are thinking about it. I believe the definition of poetry is subjective. It can be a single word, or a 50,000 line epic tale of free verse, or a painting, a glance, a film, a photograph, a sculpture, an amazing design, a play, a lover, a glass of milk or the glint in your children's eyes. Poetry is life and vice versa. I hope you enjoy these poems. I wrote some of them in college 25 years ago, but most of them were written in the intervening years. When I first sit down to write a poem I try not to think and let the words flow out in a very short period of time without stopping, or editing myself, an exercise in capturing the essence of the subconscious. Then I go back and revise it, sometimes once, sometimes a thousand times. I am loath to categorize my own art, but I would best describe this collection as metaphysical, sci-fi poetry. Imagine you are sleeping on the rings of Saturn inside a life-pod that could keep you alive for thousands of years. Enjoy.

Sincerely,
Kelvin C. Bias

Special thanks to Susan Terris of *Spillway*.
"Whispers of a Dying Sun" first appeared in *Spillway #25*

OTHER WORK BY KELVIN C. BIAS

MILKMAN (Novel)

What happens when everyman Calder Boyd starts to lactate? The Manhattanite becomes a media cause célèbre nicknamed the Milkman and old and new problems spill forth. The son of a former NBA star and a Norwegian artist, Calder copes with his strained marriage, losing his copywriting job at a boutique ad agency, a male-empowerment espousing mailman and a porn-star performance artist who wants to exploit him. He also deals with his late father's legacy and his wife's past indiscretion—all while breastfeeding their newborn daughter. Calder eventually becomes a pawn in the battle between a feminist organization and a militant men's society as he tries to become a better husband and man. The Fourth Estate, sex, art, love, memory, marriage and family converge during the snowiest winter on record in this commentary on contemporary American fatherhood.

ABOUT THE AUTHOR

Kelvin C. Bias is a journalist, filmmaker and raconteur. However, his most important moniker is father. He lives in New York City with his wife and daughters.

Whispers of a Dying Sun is his first poetry collection.

Connect with Kelvin on Instagram & Twitter: @ArchiveZero

www.ingramcontent.com/pod-product-compliance
Lightning Source LLC
Chambersburg PA
CBHW052134010526
44113CB00036B/2243